Grapeseed Press
1661 W 36th Pl
Los Angeles CA 90018
www.GrapeSeedPress.com
info@GrapeSeedPress.com

For information about special discounts available for bulk purchases, sales, promotions, fundraising, and educational needs, contact Grapeseed Press Sales at info@GrapeSeedPress.com

Cover by Nefra Rolle

Book ISBN: 978-1-958241-00-4 (Soft Cover)

Printed in the United States of America
First Printing June 2021

How To Use This Journal

Welcome! Let's get started with the
Flowers For God Gratitude Journal.

If you will set aside as little as five minutes a day, this gratitude journal provides writing prompts and inspirational Bible verses to help you find and reignite the joy, peace, love and gratitude in your life.

Complete one page each day. The most ideal time is first thing in the morning before worries, fear, doubt or the concerns of life begin pulling on you. Your thoughts will be fresh and unaffected by life's stressors.

Write from your heart. The more honest and vulnerable you are, the more you will benefit from this book. Don't be afraid to express your true feelings. There are no right or wrong answers, and no answer is too simple. If you are thankful for your morning cup of coffee, write about that.

Finally, focus on the good. The devil is trying to steal your joy. You may find your peace and joy under attack. No matter what happens throughout the day, remember:

Philippians 4:8, NLT
Do not be anxious about anything, but in every situation, by prayer and petition, with thanksgiving, present your requests to God. And the peace of God, which transcends all understanding, will guard your hearts and your minds in Christ Jesus.

But thank God! **HE** *has made us his* **CAPTIVES &** **CONTINUES TO LEAD US ALONG** **IN CHRIST'S TRIUMPHAL PROCESSION.** **NOW HE USES US** *to spread the knowledge of Christ everywhere,* **LIKE A SWEET PERFUME.** **OUR LIVES ARE A** **CHRIST-LIKE FRAGRANCE** **RISING UP** *to God.*

2 Corinthians 2:14-15a, NLT

This book belongs to:

If lost, please call or email:

Author's Note

God the Father desires for us to be so joyful, prosperous and peaceful while resting in the knowledge of Christ that our lives become a triumphal procession...a lavish celebratory parade proclaiming our victories and salvation in Christ. Our praise, thanksgiving, adoration and joy rises up to heaven like a fragrant perfume.

Our joy, praises and thanksgiving are contagious and spread to those around us, changing the atmosphere. The beautiful fragrance even reaches heaven as a sweet perfume, a gift we can send to God. I created this book for those who desire more joy, more peace and more love. These are all things that, in their fullness, come directly from God. May each page be its own unique bouquet of flowers for God.

I pray that this journal helps to reaffirm how loved you are, how much God desires to bless you and who you are in Christ. Let every prompt open your eyes and heart to hear God's voice more clearly. May the peace of Christ rest over you and your family all the days of your life.
In Jesus' name, amen.

60 DAYS OF

Peace
Joy
Gratitude
AND
God's Love

My Gratitude Goals

MAKE THE NEXT 60 DAYS COUNT

Let's figure out what your main goal is.

What is lacking in your life? Peace, Joy, Gratitude, God's Love etc

How clearly and how often do you hear from god?

1 2 3 4 5

NEVER   EVERYDAY

Do you struggle to see the good in people or Circumstances?

1 2 3 4 5

NEVER   EVERYDAY

How often do you over indulge in gossip, lose track of time on social media, binge your favorite tv show or over sleep?

1 2 3 4 5

NEVER   EVERYDAY

What do I want to accomplish over the next 60 days?

What's your long term spiritual goal for the next 6 months?

What is 1 additional thing you can do daily or weekly to bring you closer to your goal? i.e. Read the Bible daily, pray every morning etc

PSALM 9:1, NIV

I will give thanks to you, Lord, with all my heart;
I will tell of all your wonderful deeds.

Date:

Today I want to thank God for:

Write or draw anything for which you are grateful in the space below.
If you can't think of something, thank God in advance for answering a recent prayer.

Something wonderful that God has done in my life is...

PSALM 118:22-24, NIV

The stone the builders rejected has become the cornerstone; the LORD has done this, and it is marvelous in our eyes. The LORD has done it this very day; let us rejoice today and be glad.

Date:

Today I want to thank God for:

Write or draw anything for which you are grateful in the space below.
If you can't think of something, thank God in advance for answering a recent prayer.

One thing I love about myself is...

PROVERBS 16:7, NLT

When people's lives please the Lord,
even their enemies are at peace with them.

Date:

Today I want to thank God for:

Write or draw anything for which you are grateful in the space below.
If you can't think of something, thank God in advance for answering a recent prayer.

God has given me peace in this area of life:

PSALM 7:17, NIV

I will give thanks to the Lord because of his righteousness;
I will sing the praises of the name of the Lord Most High.

Date:

Today I want to thank God for:

Write or draw anything for which you are grateful in the space below.
If you can't think of something, thank God in advance for answering a recent prayer.

I am grateful to God for giving me the ability to...

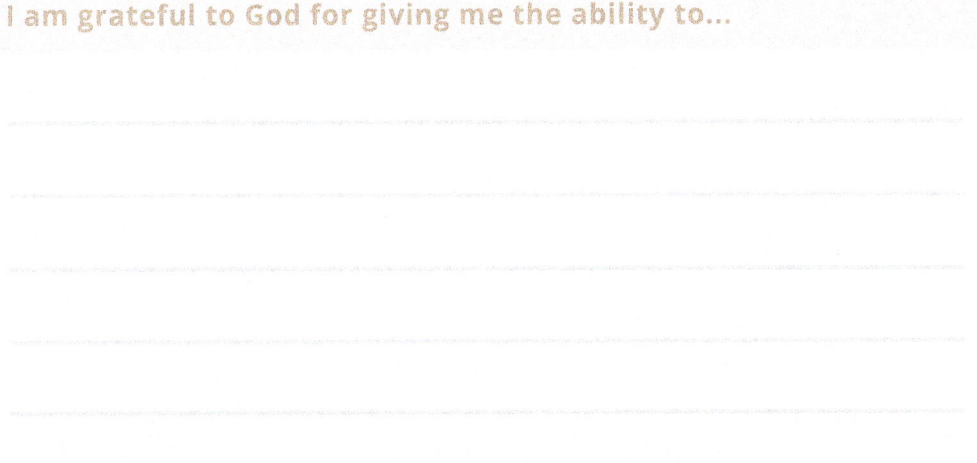

PHILIPPIANS 4:4, NIV

Rejoice in the Lord always. I will say it again: Rejoice!

Date:

Today I want to thank God for:

Write or draw anything for which you are grateful in the space below.
If you can't think of something, thank God in advance for answering a recent prayer.

One thing in my life that brings me joy is...

ISAIAH 26:3, NKJV

You will keep him in perfect peace, whose mind
is stayed on You, because he trusts in You.

Date:

Today I want to thank God for:

Write or draw anything for which you are grateful in the space below.
If you can't think of something, thank God in advance for answering a recent prayer.

In a perfect world, I would...

PSALM 95:1, NIV

Come, let us sing for joy to the Lord;
let us shout aloud to the Rock of our salvation.

Date:

Today I want to thank God for:

Write or draw anything for which you are grateful in the space below.
If you can't think of something, thank God in advance for answering a recent prayer.

In my home, I am thankful for...

PSALM 5:11, NIV

But let all who take refuge in you be glad; let them ever sing for joy. Spread your protection over them, that those who love your name may rejoice in you.

Date:

Today I want to thank God for:

Write or draw anything for which you are grateful in the space below.
If you can't think of something, thank God in advance for answering a recent prayer.

I have the most joy when I am...

JOHN 14:27, NKJV

Peace I leave with you, My peace I give to you;
not as the world gives do I give to you. Let not your
heart be troubled, neither let it be afraid.

Date:

Today I want to thank God for:

Write or draw anything for which you are grateful in the space below.
If you can't think of something, thank God in advance for answering a recent prayer.

Recently, I smiled or laughed when...

PSALM 35:18, NIV

I will give you thanks in the great assembly;
among the throngs I will praise you.

Date:

Today I want to thank God for:

Write or draw anything for which you are grateful in the space below.
If you can't think of something, thank God in advance for answering a recent prayer.

I am thankful for these material possessions:

ROMANS 14:17, NIV

For the kingdom of God is not a matter of eating and drinking, but of righteousness, peace and joy in the Holy Spirit,

Date:

Today I want to thank God for:

Write or draw anything for which you are grateful in the space below.
If you can't think of something, thank God in advance for answering a recent prayer.

I appreciate (who?) because (why?).

JOHN 16:33, NKJV

These things I have spoken to you, that in Me you
may have peace. In the world you will have tribulation;
but be of good cheer, I have overcome the world.

Date:

Today I want to thank God for:

Write or draw anything for which you are grateful in the space below.
If you can't think of something, thank God in advance for answering a recent prayer.

Recently, at my job, I enjoyed...

PSALM 106:1, NIV

Praise the Lord.
Give thanks to the Lord, for he is good;
his love endures forever.

Date:

Today I want to thank God for:

Write or draw anything for which you are grateful in the space below.
If you can't think of something, thank God in advance for answering a recent prayer.

In my life, I am thankful that others have (done what?).

3 JOHN 3-4, NIV

It gave me great joy when some believers came and testified about your faithfulness to the truth, telling how you continue to walk in it. I have no greater joy than to hear that my children are walking in the truth.

Date:

Today I want to thank God for:

Write or draw anything for which you are grateful in the space below.
If you can't think of something, thank God in advance for answering a recent prayer.

My happiest memory from my childhood is...

LEVITICUS 26:6, NKJV

I will give peace in the land, and you shall lie down, and none
will make you afraid; I will rid the land of evil beasts,
and the sword will not go through your land.

Date:

Write or draw anything for which you are grateful in the space below.
If you can't think of something, thank God in advance for answering a recent prayer.

In nature, I am inspired by (what?) and (why?).

EPHESIANS 5:19-20, NIV

Speaking to one another with psalms, hymns, and songs from the Spirit.
Sing and make music from your heart to the Lord, always giving thanks to
God the Father for everything, in the name of our Lord Jesus Christ.

Date:

Today I want to thank God for:

Write or draw anything for which you are grateful in the space below.
If you can't think of something, thank God in advance for answering a recent prayer.

I am thankful for the opportunity to be able to help people by...

JOHN 16:24, NIV

Until now you have not asked for anything in my name.
Ask and you will receive, and your joy will be complete.

Date:

Today I want to thank God for:

Write or draw anything for which you are grateful in the space below.
If you can't think of something, thank God in advance for answering a recent prayer.

I feel the most joy when I am involved in...

NUMBERS 6:26, NKJV

The LORD lift up His countenance upon you,
and give you peace.

Date:

Today I want to thank God for:

Write or draw anything for which you are grateful in the space below.
If you can't think of something, thank God in advance for answering a recent prayer.

What I love the most about my personality is...

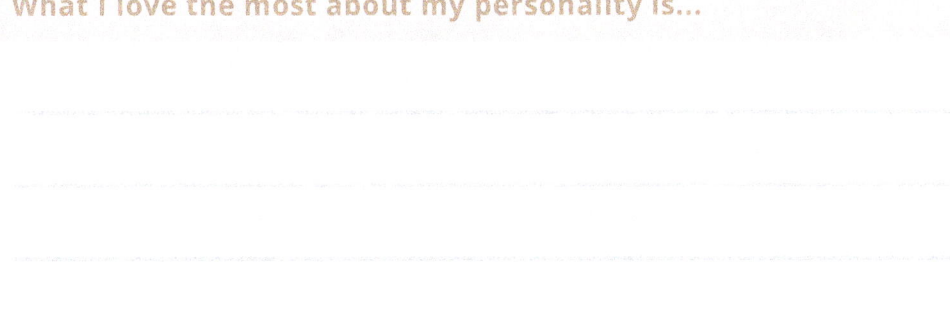

PSALM 107:21-22, NIV

Let them give thanks to the Lord for his unfailing love
and his wonderful deeds for mankind. Let them sacrifice thank
offerings and tell of his works with songs of joy.

Date:

Today I want to thank God for:

Write or draw anything for which you are grateful in the space below.
If you can't think of something, thank God in advance for answering a recent prayer.

I am thankful for my relationship(s) with...

ROMANS 12:12, NIV

Be joyful in hope, patient in affliction, faithful in prayer.

Date:

Today I want to thank God for:

Write or draw anything for which you are grateful in the space below.
If you can't think of something, thank God in advance for answering a recent prayer.

I'm grateful for this life experience:

PSALM 4:8, NKJV

I will both lie down in peace, and sleep;
for You alone, O LORD, make me dwell in safety.

Date:

Today I want to thank God for:

Write or draw anything for which you are grateful in the space below.
If you can't think of something, thank God in advance for answering a recent prayer.

I feel safe because...

COLOSSIANS 4:2, NLT

Devote yourselves to prayer with an
alert mind and a thankful heart.

Date:

Write or draw anything for which you are grateful in the space below.
If you can't think of something, thank God in advance for answering a recent prayer.

My life has been improved recently because I have learned...

22

JAMES 1:2-3, NIV

Consider it pure joy, my brothers and sisters, whenever
you face trials of many kinds, because you know that
the testing of your faith produces perseverance.

Date:

Today I want to thank God for:

Write or draw anything for which you are grateful in the space below.
If you can't think of something, thank God in advance for answering a recent prayer.

The biggest obstacle in life that I have overcome is...

PSALM 37:11, KJV

But the meek shall inherit the earth, and shall delight themselves in the abundance of peace.

Date:

Today I want to thank God for:

Write or draw anything for which you are grateful in the space below.
If you can't think of something, thank God in advance for answering a recent prayer.

The most peaceful place I know of is...

PSALM 118:1, NIV

Give thanks to the Lord, for he is good;
his love endures forever.

Date:

Today I want to thank God for:

Write or draw anything for which you are grateful in the space below.
If you can't think of something, thank God in advance for answering a recent prayer.

I am thankful that (what?) is different today than it was a year ago.

ACTS 2:28, NLT

You have shown me the way of life,
and you will fill me with the joy of your presence.'

Date:

Write or draw anything for which you are grateful in the space below.
If you can't think of something, thank God in advance for answering a recent prayer.

My perfect life would be...

PSALM 55:18, NKJV

He has redeemed my soul in peace from the
battle that was against me, for there were many against me.

Date:

Write or draw anything for which you are grateful in the space below.
If you can't think of something, thank God in advance for answering a recent prayer.

My favorite memory from the past ten years is...

PSALM 69:30, NLT

Then I will praise God's name with singing,
and I will honor him with thanksgiving.

Date:

Today I want to thank God for:

Write or draw anything for which you are grateful in the space below.
If you can't think of something, thank God in advance for answering a recent prayer.

I'm thankful for the opportunity I had/have to...

PROVERBS 10:28, NTL

The hopes of the godly result in happiness,
but the expectations of the wicked come to nothing.

Date:

Today I want to thank God for:

Write or draw anything for which you are grateful in the space below.
If you can't think of something, thank God in advance for answering a recent prayer.

Something fun that I look forward to doing is...

PROVERBS 3:2-3, NKJV

For length of days and long life and peace they will add to you.
Let not mercy and truth forsake you; bind them
around your neck; write them on the tablet of your heart.

Date:

Today I want to thank God for:

Write or draw anything for which you are grateful in the space below.
If you can't think of something, thank God in advance for answering a recent prayer.

One thing I love about my physical appearance is...

ROMANS 5:5, NLT

And this hope will not lead to disappointment. For we know how dearly God loves us, because he has given us the Holy Spirit to fill our hearts with his love.

Date:

Today I want to thank God for:

Write or draw anything for which you are grateful in the space below.
If you can't think of something, thank God in advance for answering a recent prayer.

I am grateful for these experiences:

PSALM 36:5-6, NLT

Your unfailing love, O LORD, is as vast as the heavens; your faithfulness reaches beyond the clouds. Your righteousness is like the mighty mountains, your justice like the ocean depths. You care for people and animals alike, O LORD.

Date:

Today I want to thank God for:

Write or draw anything for which you are grateful in the space below.
If you can't think of something, thank God in advance for answering a recent prayer.

I felt the most loved when I had this experience:

ISAIAH 52:7, NLT

How beautiful on the mountains
are the feet of the messenger who brings good news,
the good news of peace and salvation,
the news that the God of Israel[a] reigns!

Date:

Today I want to thank God for:

Write or draw anything for which you are grateful in the space below.
If you can't think of something, thank God in advance for answering a recent prayer.

If I were on top of Mt. Everest, one thing I would yell to the world is...

ROMANS 15:13, NLT

I pray that God, the source of hope, will fill you
completely with joy and peace because you trust in
him. Then you will overflow with confident hope
through the power of the Holy Spirit.

Date:

Today I want to thank God for:

Write or draw anything for which you are grateful in the space below.
If you can't think of something, thank God in advance for answering a recent prayer.

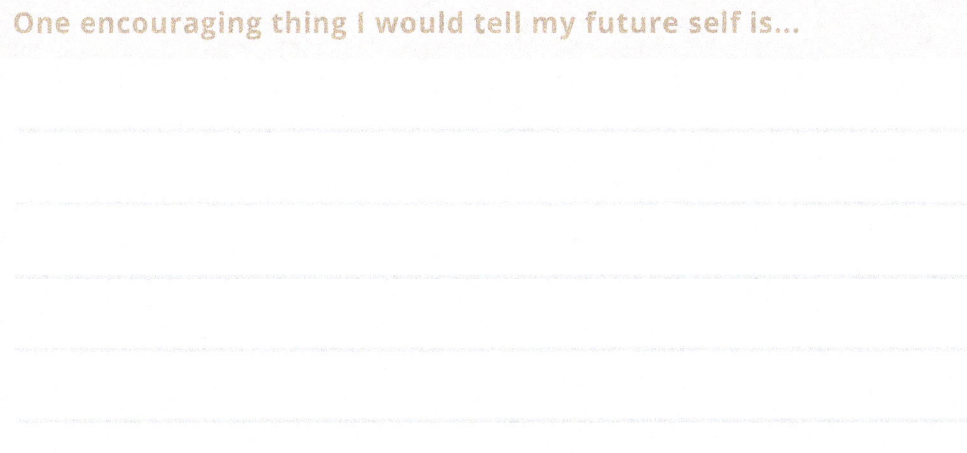

One encouraging thing I would tell my future self is...

PSALM 147:7, NIV

Sing to the Lord with grateful praise;
make music to our God on the harp.

Date:

Write or draw anything for which you are grateful in the space below.
If you can't think of something, thank God in advance for answering a recent prayer.

I am grateful for the insights I have gained about...

JEREMIAH 29:11, NKJV

For I know the thoughts that I think toward you, says the LORD, thoughts of peace and not of evil, to give you a future and a hope.

Date:

Today I want to thank God for:

Write or draw anything for which you are grateful in the space below.
If you can't think of something, thank God in advance for answering a recent prayer.

My perfect future would be...

JOHN 15:11, NLT

I have told you these things so that you will be filled
with my joy. Yes, your joy will overflow!

Date:

Today I want to thank God for:

Write or draw anything for which you are grateful in the space below.
If you can't think of something, thank God in advance for answering a recent prayer.

The last compliment I remember receiving was...

DANIEL 2:23, NLT

I thank and praise you, God of my ancestors, for you have given me wisdom and strength. You have told me what we asked of you and revealed to us what the king demanded."

Date:

Today I want to thank God for:

Write or draw anything for which you are grateful in the space below.
If you can't think of something, thank God in advance for answering a recent prayer.

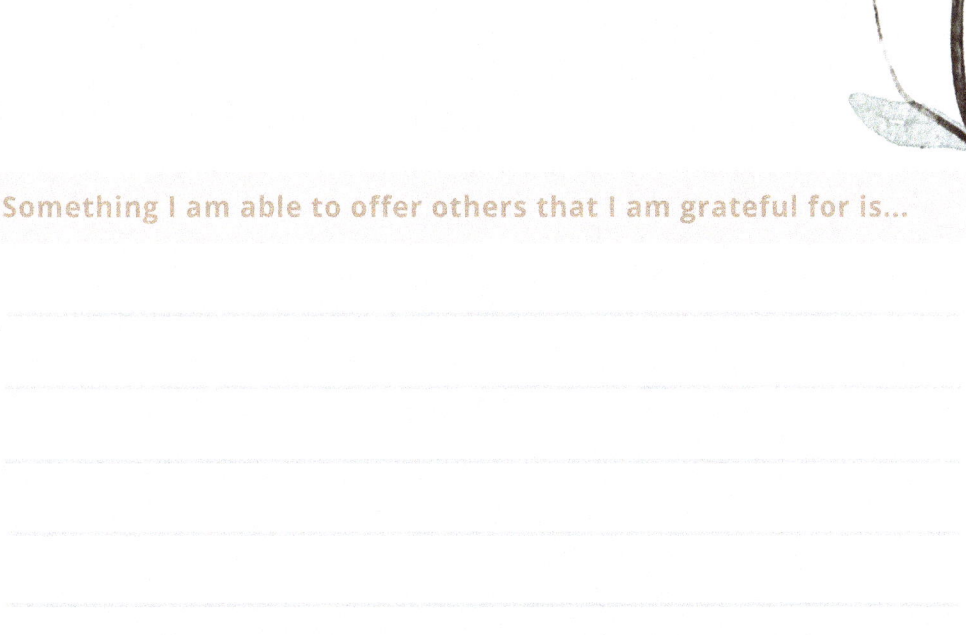

Something I am able to offer others that I am grateful for is...

MARK 4:39, NKJV

Then He arose and rebuked the wind, and said to the sea,
'Peace, be still!' And the wind ceased and there was a great calm.

Date:

Today I want to thank God for:

Write or draw anything for which you are grateful in the space below.
If you can't think of something, thank God in advance for answering a recent prayer.

The one thing I would do to make the world a better place is...

PSALM 100:4-5, NLT

Enter his gates with thanksgiving; go into his courts with praise.
Give thanks to him and praise his name. For the Lord is good.
His unfailing love continues forever,
and his faithfulness continues to each generation.

Date:

Today I want to thank God for:

Write or draw anything for which you are grateful in the space below.
If you can't think of something, thank God in advance for answering a recent prayer.

In past generations of my family, I'm thankful that...

ROMANS 12:15, NLT

Be happy with those who are happy,
and weep with those who weep.

Date:

Write or draw anything for which you are grateful in the space below.
If you can't think of something, thank God in advance for answering a recent prayer.

I love to be around (who?) because...

41

LUKE 1:79, NKJV

To give light to those who sit in darkness and the shadow
of death, to guide our feet into the way of peace.

Date:

Today I want to thank God for:

Write or draw anything for which you are grateful in the space below.
If you can't think of something, thank God in advance for answering a recent prayer.

(Who?) has been a great role model in my life by...

PHILIPPIANS 4:6-7, NLT

Don't worry about anything; instead, pray about everything.
Tell God what you need, and thank him for all he has done. Then
you will experience God's peace, which exceeds anything we can understand.
His peace will guard your hearts and minds as you live in Christ Jesus.

Date:

Today I want to thank God for:

Write or draw anything for which you are grateful in the space below.
If you can't think of something, thank God in advance for answering a recent prayer.

In this very moment, I can be grateful for...

GALATIANS 5:22, NIV

But the fruit of the Spirit is love, joy, peace,
forbearance, kindness, goodness, faithfulness,

Date:

Today I want to thank God for:

Write or draw anything for which you are grateful in the space below.
If you can't think of something, thank God in advance for answering a recent prayer.

One thing I have done to help those I love is...

ROMANS 5:1, NKJV

Therefore, having been justified by faith, we have
peace with God through our Lord Jesus Christ.

Date:

Today I want to thank God for:

Write or draw anything for which you are grateful in the space below.
If you can't think of something, thank God in advance for answering a recent prayer.

The most peaceful place I can imagine looks and sounds like...

COLOSSIANS 2:6-7, NIV

So then, just as you received Christ Jesus as Lord, continue to live your lives in him, rooted and built up in him, strengthened in the faith as you were taught, and overflowing with thankfulness.

Date:

Today I want to thank God for:

Write or draw anything for which you are grateful in the space below.
If you can't think of something, thank God in advance for answering a recent prayer.

As I look around me right now, I can be grateful for...

PSALM 126:5-6, NIV
Those who sow with tears will reap with songs of joy.
Those who go out weeping, carrying seed to sow,
will return with songs of joy, carrying sheaves with them.

Date:

Today I want to thank God for:

Write or draw anything for which you are grateful in the space below.
If you can't think of something, thank God in advance for answering a recent prayer.

One thing I love about myself is...

ROMANS 8:6, KJV

For to be carnally minded is death,
but to be spiritually minded is life and peace.

Date:

Today I want to thank God for:

Write or draw anything for which you are grateful in the space below.
If you can't think of something, thank God in advance for answering a recent prayer.

If I had no limitations, financial or otherwise, I would...

PSALM 31:7, NLT

I will be glad and rejoice in your unfailing love, for you have seen my troubles, and you care about the anguish of my soul.

Date:

Today I want to thank God for:

Write or draw anything for which you are grateful in the space below.
If you can't think of something, thank God in advance for answering a recent prayer.

One thing I love about my life since accepting Christ is...

ISAIAH 61:10, NIV

I delight greatly in the LORD; my soul rejoices in my God. For he has clothed me with garments of salvation and arrayed me in a robe of his righteousness, as a bridegroom adorns his head like a priest, and as a bride adorns herself with her jewels.

Date:

Today I want to thank God for:

Write or draw anything for which you are grateful in the space below.
If you can't think of something, thank God in advance for answering a recent prayer.

Though I normally take it for granted, I am very grateful for...

JOSHUA 1:9, NIV

Have I not commanded you? Be strong and courageous.
Do not be afraid; do not be discouraged, for the LORD
your God will be with you wherever you go."

Date:

Today I want to thank God for:

Write or draw anything for which you are grateful in the space below.
If you can't think of something, thank God in advance for answering a recent prayer.

The most courageous thing I've ever done or said is...

PSALM 109:26, NIV

Help me, LORD my God; save me
according to your unfailing love.

Date:

Today I want to thank God for:

Write or draw anything for which you are grateful in the space below.
If you can't think of something, thank God in advance for answering a recent prayer.

The last time God saved me from something was...

PSALM 71:23, NIV

My lips will shout for joy when I sing praise to you—
I whom you have delivered.

Date:

Write or draw anything for which you are grateful in the space below.
If you can't think of something, thank God in advance for answering a recent prayer.

One challenge that God helped me overcome or delivered me from is...

1 CORINTHIANS 14:33, NKJV

For God is not the author of confusion but of peace,
as in all the churches of the saints.

Date:

Today I want to thank God for:

Write or draw anything for which you are grateful in the space below.
If you can't think of something, thank God in advance for answering a recent prayer.

If a book were written about me, I would want people to know...

HEBREWS 12:28-29, NIV

Therefore, since we are receiving a kingdom that cannot be shaken,
let us be thankful, and so worship God acceptably with
reverence and awe, for our "God is a consuming fire."

Date:

Today I want to thank God for:

Write or draw anything for which you are grateful in the space below.
If you can't think of something, thank God in advance for answering a recent prayer.

My life is made easier because of...

PSALM 16:11, NIV

You make known to me the path of life; you will fill me with joy in your presence, with eternal pleasures at your right hand.

Date:

Today I want to thank God for:

Write or draw anything for which you are grateful in the space below.
If you can't think of something, thank God in advance for answering a recent prayer.

One life goal that I have already achieved is...

2 CORINTHIANS 13:11, NKJV

Finally, brethren, farewell. Become complete.
Be of good comfort, be of one mind, live in peace;
and the God of love and peace will be with you.

Date:

Today I want to thank God for:

Write or draw anything for which you are grateful in the space below.
If you can't think of something, thank God in advance for answering a recent prayer.

Simple activities that bring me comfort are...

HEBREWS 13:15-16, NIV

Through Jesus, therefore, let us continually offer to God a
sacrifice of praise — the fruit of lips that openly profess his
name. And do not forget to do good and to share with others,
for with such sacrifices God is pleased.

Date:

Today I want to thank God for:

Write or draw anything for which you are grateful in the space below.
If you can't think of something, thank God in advance for answering a recent prayer.

Sacrifices that I have made in life that resulted in good are...

1 JOHN 4:7, NIV

Dear friends, let us love one another, for love comes from God.
Everyone who loves has been born of God and knows God.

Date:

Today I want to thank God for:

Write or draw anything for which you are grateful in the space below.
If you can't think of something, thank God in advance for answering a recent prayer.

The greatest act of love I have experienced is...

COLOSSIANS 3:15, NKJV

And let the peace of God rule in your hearts, to which
also you were called in one body; and be thankful.

Date:

Today I want to thank God for:

Write or draw anything for which you are grateful in the space below.
If you can't think of something, thank God in advance for answering a recent prayer.

One relationship that fills my heart with joy is...

Congratulations
YOU DID IT!

You just completed 60 days of gratitude.

Visit the Godtivity Creative Christian Wellness Shop

All the products in our shop have been hand-picked to blend Christian beliefs with beauty and wellness. We use the highest quality ingredients with an emphasis on natural and plant-based products. Everything here is designed to make living a healthy and devoted life easier by using Biblical truths to enhance both your life, your health and your connection to God.

Visit Shop

Created To Create

God's creative spirit lives in you.

**Increase your creative ability and open
yourself up to hear from God today.**

Introducing: 21 Days Of Prayer, Peace & God's Presence

<mark>**A Daniel Fast For Creative Christians**</mark>

7 Day Fast +
Self Care Kit

21 Day Fast +
Self Care Kit

Thank You

I AM EXTREMELY GRATEFUL FOR YOU!

Thank you for purchasing this gratitude journal.
I am extremely grateful and hope you found value in
using it. Please consider sharing it with friends or
family and leaving an awesome ★ ★ ★ ★ ★ review
online. Your feedback and support are always
appreciated, and allow me to continue creating
resources, tools and products for believers
everywhere.

With Peace & Love,

Nefra

God's creative spirit lives in you.

**Do not despise these small beginnings,
for the LORD rejoices to see the work begin...**

Zechariah 4:10 NLT

NOTES